YOUR KNOWLEDGE HAS VALUE

- We will publish your bachelor's and
  master's thesis, essays and papers

- Your own eBook and book -
  sold worldwide in all relevant shops

- Earn money with each sale

Upload your text at www.GRIN.com
and publish for free

Moissej Sverdlin

Tasks of a community manager

GRIN Publishing

Bibliographic information published by the German National Library:

The German National Library lists this publication in the National Bibliography; detailed bibliographic data are available on the Internet at http://dnb.dnb.de .

This book is copyright material and must not be copied, reproduced, transferred, distributed, leased, licensed or publicly performed or used in any way except as specifically permitted in writing by the publishers, as allowed under the terms and conditions under which it was purchased or as strictly permitted by applicable copyright law. Any unauthorized distribution or use of this text may be a direct infringement of the author s and publisher s rights and those responsible may be liable in law accordingly.

Imprint:

Copyright © 2005 GRIN Verlag GmbH
Print and binding: Books on Demand GmbH, Norderstedt Germany
ISBN: 978-3-656-82614-9

This book at GRIN:

http://www.grin.com/en/e-book/63737/tasks-of-a-community-manager

GRIN - Your knowledge has value

Since its foundation in 1998, GRIN has specialized in publishing academic texts by students, college teachers and other academics as e-book and printed book. The website www.grin.com is an ideal platform for presenting term papers, final papers, scientific essays, dissertations and specialist books.

Visit us on the internet:

http://www.grin.com/

http://www.facebook.com/grincom

http://www.twitter.com/grin_com

Technische Universität München
Fakultät für Informatik
Lehrstuhl für Wirtschaftsinformatik (I 17)

Seminararbeit

Proseminar im 2. Semester

Virtuelle Communities

Thema: Tasks of a community manager

Wirtschaftsinformatik im 2. Semester

Eingereicht am 20. Mai 2005

Tasks of a Community Manager

Structure of the paper:

1. Introductionary words about Virtual Communities

The Internet has evolved in the last 15 years in such a speed and in such a mass that the world has changed dramatically. If in the year 1985 a normal West German student would have wanted to learn about new developments in the world he had watched news in the television or had read a newspaper. But if he wanted more specific information about something then there were no means left. Today at every minute of the day in every city of the world {with Iridium Satelite Phone coverage, it is possible to get an Internet connection at every point of the world} [www.iridium.com , accessed on the 18th of May 2005] every human being can receive every information she or he desires. We are in the information society!

That information we require can come from different sources. It can be trusted news service like CNN [www.cnn.com], a well known encyclopedia e.g. the Encyclopedia Encarta [www.encarta.com] or a rather informal source e.g. a virtual community like Well [www.well.com]...

Wait a moment! You might ask yourself why after the most famous news network and the largest encyclopedia in the world I have mentioned a virtual community... The answer is clear → the internet has evolved so much that today it is possible to get almost every answer you want from almost every specialist you want for free! [Concept from: Rheingold 1993, chapter 1]

What does it mean? It means that millions and millions of internet users are exchanging their thoughts and combining their knowledge for an exchange of information

2. Declaration of my research question

As the subject of my paper is the "tasks of a community manager" I have thought which aspects of the work of a community manager would be an interesting subject for this study. Traditionally a management position is a position which requires academic knowledge; trust from the subordinates and a responsibility for the company and its employees. In the case of a virtual community manager, those three aspects are still the same. Since trust in virtual communities is part of another paper and erudite knowledge in the area of community managing is a very well spread area, the aim of the following 6 pages will be to answer my question:

"What are the responsibilities a Community Manager has to take care of?"

3. Classification of virtual communities

In the last 15 years since the first VC (WELL – Whole Earth 'Lectronic Link, a huge community of people around the world discussing topics 24/7 [concept from Rheingold 1993, chapter 1] many communities have been created and many have been diminished for many reasons be it loss of interest or loss of financial capabilities. Evolutions in the WWW lead to more distinctness in the communities. Several categories have evolved by that process and so a VC has to be classified in order for a scientific glance on it.

3.1 Definition of a virtual community

A "Virtual Community", a term invented by Howard Rheingold in his book "The Virtual Community" 1993, is a group of people who are connected online to each other by one equal interest. As there are several different kinds of virtual communities the ties may be more or less closer.

Derek M. Powazek the author of "Design for Community knows three kinds of virtual communities:
- Communities of support
- Communities of shared stories
- Communities of commerce

Communities of support are communities in which common people share their experiences with their own diseases or those of their close ones.
Communities of shared stories are used to tell personal stories and to receive feedback from other human beings to one self's problems and events in life.
Communities of commerce center the idea of a company to promote their products or their brand name by inviting users to share their experiences with those products or brands online.
[Powazek 2001, 136-142]

3.2 Work areas in virtual communities

There are four work areas in virtual communities:
- Moderating
- Technical Supervision
- Designing
- Financing

Usually VCs have some kind of communicating platform. This could be either a moderated chat {a platform to write live messages to each other, while the whole communication is monitored by a moderator for profanities}, an unmediated chat {same like a moderated chat with the exception that the conversations are not controlled}, or a bulletin board {a platform in which users can write about certain topics, other users can see those messages and respond to them}.

3.3 Human Resources infrastructure of a virtual community

A VC's human resources infrastructure has the form of a pyramid. In the lowest level there are the normal members. They are the ones on which the community consists on. Over the normal members are the enthusiastic members, who are very much in touch with community. Above them are the honorary employees of a VC. They moderate, design or program for the community for free. On top of them are paid employees of a community, note that paid employees are rather rare in the Internet. Th reason for that is that only few VCs have the funding to pay employees on a constant basis. They are professionals who lead teams of honorary employees or are responsible for the technical side of a VC, for details read 4.2. Above all personel is the community manager. He is responsible for all employees, for financial oversight and for the policies of the VC. [Kim 2001, 175]

4. Needs of virtual communities

Every VC has its own prerequisite for a successful ongoing activity of its own. First there come the monetary requirements without which the community could not be sustained online. After that technological needs come about on whose the community platform is based on. Last there are the social elements of a VC without there would be no community.

4.1 Financial Needs

There are several expense factors which play a roll for virtual communities. The first of those is computer hardware & software that is crucial for running an online community. Second is the web space which is needed to upload data on the internet for the website to be viewable for the end user. Following is the traffic, the amount of data send between the server and the users. As there are different types of virtual communities, wages for the personal who are working for the virtual community can be a potential factor as well. [Concept of Powazek 2001, 226-227]

In most cases of virtual communities the Server and the applications for the use of the communities is outsourced to a company specialized on hosting Internet Pages and its content. Only big companies (e.g. BMW www.bmw.de) who have their own IT department and servers usually use their own computer resources for accommodating the corporate online community or in BMW's case its Intranet (the in-house only internet with Webpages designed and kept updated by and for BMW employees).

4.1.1 Advertisements

Advertisements are the most common way of financement. Money flows into the VC by banners, rectangles on the page in which is an advertisement of a company, and by clicking on it you are forwarded to the company's web site.

4.1.2 Merchandising

Larger communities with many members can get funding by merchandising products with the logo or other motifs of the VC. Typical products are mugs or t-shirts.

4.1.3. Donations

Users of a community who like it and want to support it can contribute to the VC by making a donation. There are several VCs who combine donations with a "premium" account in the VC, e.g. www.telefon-treff.de. Such premium members usually do not have to see any advertisements or have no storage limits in the on site private message account (Found out by own experiences and research)

4.1.4. Budget

Business communities or corporate Intranet communities usually have a budget by which the VC is financed. Those communities normally are the best funded type of communities on the net.

4.2 Technological Needs

A programmer who is able to write the code for the VC databases, in which the data of the members or other personal input is saved, or the VC site itself is needed. Smaller communities (e.g. Telefon Treff – a huge nonprofit VC based on Telecommunication / www.telefon-treff.de) use standardized products which are already available on the web because of the low budget of most non commerce VC's. After the software there is the hardware platform. Servers for the accessibility of the site are needed because every user who wishes to reach the web site sends requests to it and through these requests he gets answers which usually are the web pages the user can see at the end. For these requests a lot of computational power is needed which is why a server is required. Many communities offer bulletin boards, electronic message centers in which every member posts messages to specific topics, or private messages, on-the-platform emails which are exchanged between registered users of the community. Both functionalities require storage capacity that has to be provided by the VC.

4.3 Social Needs

Community is by definition:

> ".. a set of people (or agents in a more abstract sense) with some shared element ..."
> [http://en.wikipedia.org/wiki/Community , accessed on May the 18th 2005].

That said it means that a VC requires first of all humans who are interested in using it and second of all a common attraction which combines them all together.
Depending on the kind of VC members tend to share very personal facts of their lives which normally they would only tell to closest friends and families:

> "Woods Hole. Midnight. I am sitting in the dark of my daughter's room. Her monitor lights blink at me. The lights used to blink too brightly so I covered them with bits of bandage adhesive and now they flash faintly underneath, a persistent red and green, Lillie's heart and lungs. Above the monitor is her portable suction unit. In the glow of the flashlight I'm writing by, it looks like the plastic guts of a science-class human model, the tubes coiled around the power supply, the reservoir, the pump. Tina is upstairs trying to get some sleep. A baby monitor links our bedroom to Lillie's. It links our sleep to Lillie's too, and because our souls are linked to hers, we do not sleep well. I am naked. My stomach is full of beer. The flashlight rests on it, and the beam rises and falls with my breath. My daughter breathes through a white plastic tube inserted into a hole in her throat. She's fourteen months old." [Rheingold 1993, chapter 1]

Such personal insights into another life are only possible if the trust the author of a post like that has, is big enough into the social capabilities of other members of the VC. This is typical for communities of support (see 3.1) in which people can share their perception of diseases and by that relief each other.

5. Areas of Community Managing

A community manager has many responsibilities in different areas and those responsibilities may be more or less important depending on the type of community he manages. The idea of a community is to share knowledge between humans. To support this principle the administrator has to choose a method of knowledge management and the technological means to support this method. Following the construct of knowledge management the community itself needs to be built. That implies two different things: 1. building the technological base for a community and 2. enlarging the number of members so after a period of time a community of users is created. When such a community is built usually more and more tasks come up and those need to be delegated to employees. Of course the manager is responsible for a certain level of quality of his employees so he has to keep an eye on all developments. VCs have a certain budget which needs to be controlled and skillfully used.

5.1 Knowledge Management

An important goal of in community managing is to provide the best possible enabling conditions for the members of a VC. [Beichelt 2002, 36] Those conditions are the context in which the users post their bulletins. One such factor could be to enlarge the population of a community [see 6.2] so that a question which is posted would receive an answer from a competent user. Another component is to build up the technological platform on which knowledge can be exchanged between a "questioner" and an "answerer" [Beichelt 2002, 37]. Such a platform could be a bulletin board e.g. www.telefon-treff.de or a chat (either moderated or unmediated). For knowledge management in a larger community bulletin boards have the advantage that questions and answers are visible for a long period of time and that means that a larger group of people can benefit out of one single post. [Beichelt 2002, 34 / concept partly from Beerli et al. 2003, 101-103]

5.2 Community Building

Every VC starts with one member. This first member is usually the community manager who has the idea for a new VC. He has a great concept, beautiful designed pages and a wonderful name for his community. Now he only needs one more thing…: members. The only problem is that those are not very easy to get and far harder to keep. New members need to identify themselves with the idea or theme of VC. [Kim 2001, 209]

A good example for that is a community of support like the German speaking community: Krebs Kompass [www.krebs-kompass.de]. This VC is for humans who are ill with cancer or their close ones. Information about different kinds of cancer, symptoms as well as contact to local support groups is provided as an informational part. Members or guests of the community have the possibility not only to get informed but also to share their fears or their stories of good recoveries. Through such a high grade of personalization of the community, it is based around one main theme - cancer, it is easy for a possible new member to get familiarized quickly and become a full member of the VC. [Concept from Rheingold 1993, chapter 1, concept from Renninger 2002, 60-63and my own internet research]

5.3 Supervision of Employees

After the first phase of community building – when the structure is build up and more and more users become members – the member count rises quickly. For one single person the workload will get too much and he will require help to moderate the incoming requests, delete trash topics or simply keep track of the development of the VC. Employees will need to be hired. In normal nonprofit VC those employees will usually be nonpaid honorary employees. If there will be more and more moderators then the chance of black sheep rises who could try to use their moderating powers, extra community tools which allow them e.g. to delete or move topics, for an evil aim. Such problems need to be contained and kept low. [Kim 2001, 176 / Haywood 1998, 107-109]

A good method for that was developed my Rob Malda, founder of big VC Slashdot [www.slashdot.org]. Shortly after the founding of his community it grew in a very high rate. News coverage, member registration and topic count rose quickly. Alone he could not get hold of the mass of new posts. Following that he employed honorary moderators, who should check new messages for junk. After some time even the new moderating team was overwhelmed and he thought about a new technique to control the mass of posts. The idea of constantly enrolling new moderators who needed training and control was not very favorable for him so he invented something new.

He wrote a program which chose randomly several hundreds of users who wrote good tidings. Those members, who were no moderators or any other employees, had to rate postings of other members in a grades ranging from one till 5 stars. That meant between trash and excellent literature quality. Chosen members had this special task for only a few days after which they would regain their old status of normal users. When some months passed they could be chosen again by Malda's program. [Kim 2001, 162-163]

5.4 Financial Oversight

One of the biggest responsibilities of a VC manager is financial oversight of his budget. Depending on the size of the VC the budget can range from zero, in a small nonprofit VC, to hundreds of thousands of Euros, in a company internal VC e.g. the Intranet system of the Boston Consulting Group [www.bcg.de & Reichwald et al, 2005 – guest lecture in the course of Prof. Reichwald at TUM].

This money has to be used wisely for not to be spend entirely on not crucial parts, e.g. to spend 50,000 € of a 100,000 € budget solely on the design of a VC. To ensure that something like does not happen the sender of such amounts of money want guarantees and proof that it's spend wisely and for a good cause. Because of that the budget needs to be accounted by the manager and money can only be spent after his consent.

6. Communication in Virtual Communities

VCs gain their big dynamics from the communication between its members. Everyone wants to know something and some people even want to answer the question of others or simply to react to something he or she read. This communication can take place in different ways. First there is the common way: over the platform. May it be by posting a question into a topic in a bulletin board or ask something in a chat. Second there is a method on bulletin board platforms: private messages. Private messages are platform based emails. Only members of a community can send them and the recipient can only be another recipient of the same community.

By allowing such a method of communication the community manager achieves one important task: to bound his members to the community. They do not have to use standardized emails to send messages privately to each other but can do that while using the VC. [Concept partly from Fisher 2007, 197-200]

7. Conclusion

A community manager is responsible for the whole VC. Those responsibilities range from making sure that there is enough funding for the community over enrolling a good team of employees and keeping them on track to the goals which he himself sets. You have read many examples of VCs and the relevant functions that are special about them. With those responsibilities listed in the last 7 pages and clear case models where those responsibilities where shown I hope that the question was answered satisfactionally.

Moissej Sverdlin

Munich, May the 20th 2005

8. Bibliography

- Alfred J. Beerli, Svenja Falk, Daniel Diemers: Knowledge management and networked environments: leveraging intellectual capital in virtual business communities , Publisher: New York ;London :AMACOM, 243 pages, (2003)
- Beichelt, S.: Knowledge Management in Virtual Communities. Diplomarbeit im Studiengang der Verwaltungswissenschaft an der Universität Konstanz. April 2002
- Fisher, Kimball :The distance manager : a hands-on guide to managing off-site employees and virtual teams; Publisher: New York ; London : McGraw-Hill, 252 pages, (2001)
- Haywood, Martha, Managing virtual teams : practical techniques for high-technology project managers, Boston, Mass. ; London : Artech House, 199 Pages:;; (1998)
- Kim, Amy Jo, Community Building on the Web, 352 pages, publisher: Addison Wesley, (2000)
- Powazek, Derek M., Design for Community ; Publisher: New Riders, 1st edition ; 307 pages (2001)
- K. Ann Renninger, Wesley Shuma : Building virtual communities : learning and change in cyberspace , Cambridge : Cambridge University Press, 380 pages.- cased, , (2002)
- Rheingold, Howard ; The Virtual Community: Homesteading on the Electronic Frontier, 360 pages   Publisher: The MIT Press; 1st edition (2000)
- www.telefon-treff.de , accessed on May the 18th 2005
- www.bcg.de , accessed on May the 19th 2005
- www.bmw.de, accessed on May the 19th 2005
- www.krebs-kompass.de , accessed on May the 19th 2005
- www.shashdot.org, accessed on May the 18th 2005
- www.iridium.com accessed on the 18th of May 2005